HITCHIN TOWN
THROUGH TIME
Hugh Madgin

AMBERLEY PUBLISHING

First published 2014

Amberley Publishing
The Hill, Stroud, Gloucestershire, GL5 4EP
www.amberley-books.com

Copyright © Hugh Madgin, 2014

The right of Hugh Madgin to be identified as the Author
of this work has been asserted in accordance with the
Copyrights, Designs and Patents Act 1988.

ISBN 978 1 4456 4196 6 (print)
ISBN 978 1 4456 4204 8 (ebook)

British Library Cataloguing in Publication Data.
A catalogue record for this book is available from the
British Library.

Typesetting by Amberley Publishing.
Printed in Great Britain.

Introduction

Once the second largest town in Hertfordshire, Hitchin today remains the principal town of North Hertfordshire, even if its neighbours Letchworth and Stevenage, which expanded massively during the twentieth century, are greater in size. Voted in a poll by *The Times* in 2013 as the 9th best town in the UK in which to live, Hitchin remains a flourishing town, with markets on Tuesdays, Fridays and Saturdays.

Its position on the East Coast Main Line has been crucial to its development since the mid-nineteenth century; indeed, the town rapidly expanded towards the station along Nightingale Road and what is now Walsworth Road. Today, Hitchin is a very popular commuter town, as anyone standing on the Down platform of the station in the evening peak will appreciate when a twelve-car train disgorges its hundreds of passengers.

The core of the town is based on the traditional pattern of a lengthy, ever-widening street, which is Bancroft in the north and takes in the High Street alongside infill by the Churchyard and then further infill between Sun Street and Bucklersbury. The street contains many fine buildings dating from the fifteenth century onwards. Inevitably, the second half of the twentieth century saw some demolitions that are now regretted. These include, principally, The Croft in Bancroft, the former Bull Inn at the Triangle, and the buildings between Portmill Lane and Hermitage Road in Bancroft, but many others survive and are cherished.

Much new building has taken place in the town in the past couple of decades, from new office blocks to town-centre mews developments. The latter, with some irony, replicate (albeit to a higher standard) the yards of houses built in the boom years of the nineteenth century, and which, from the 1920s, were cleared away. Such projects in the twenty-first century have generally paid great attention to their surroundings, rather than following the pattern of 1950s and 1960s planners, who wanted to stamp their authority over what had gone before.

It is impossible not to be charmed by Hitchin, a town that has changed in detail over the last hundred years but has never lost sight of its roots, as I hope these pages will show.

Hugh Madgin, 2014

Acknowledgements

The compilation of this book would have been impossible without the generous assistance of a number of people in the provision of photographs, access and information. They are: Mrs Patricia Aspinall, Wendy Cant, Laurence and Neil Chaffey, Neil Collin, Mark Seaman-Hill, Don Hills, David Hodges and Hitchin Museum, Stephen Holland, Terry Knight, Brian Norman, Richard Whitmore and Robbie Yon. Special thanks are due to my wife, Cath, for her unfailing support.

In addition to providing photographs, Terry Knight kindly proofread the manuscript. Any errors that remain are entirely my own.

About the Author

Hugh Madgin has been fascinated by Hitchin and its history for years. Other books he has produced in the *Through Time* series are *Stevenage Through Time*, *Hitchin Through Time*, *Cromer Through Time*, *Knebworth Through Time* and *Baldock Through Time*.

He is the creator of hitchinonthenet.com.

The Park and Priory

At the very apex of Hitchin society, both in social standing and size of residence, stood The Priory and its inhabitants, the Radcliffe and Delmé-Radcliffe families, who lived here for more than four centuries until 1963. Today, the park has been bisected by Hitchin's bypass, and there are new office blocks in the Priory grounds, but this attractive vista of a century ago remains.

The River Hiz, the Park

Today the banks of the River Hiz through the park are largely obscured by tree growth, which screens the blocks Keynes House, Pease House and Radcliffe House from the park. The park was used for public events, such as the Hitchin Pageant of 1951, in the days when it was the home of the Delmé-Radcliffes. In recent years, it has been the location of the Rhythms of the World festival.

Park Way

The earlier view above shows work underway to carve out the cutting for the southern end of the bypass in September 1980. A third of a century later, the trees in the background along Gosmore Road provide a reference point.

Hitchin Hill

The descent into the town from the junction of London and Stevenage roads. Since the construction of the Park Way bypass road, the truncated stub of Gosmore Road seen in the left foreground has been renamed Priory End and serves the Milford Lodge residential home.

Triangle Temperance Hotel

There have been three hotels at The Triangle: the ancient Bull Inn (a sliver of whose jettied structure can be seen on the extreme left in the earlier view), the Lord Lister Hotel and the Temperance Hotel. The Lord Lister Hotel was for many years known as Scott House, at which time it was the 'Home for Girls of Weak & Defective Intelligence'. Around twenty girls operated a laundry here under a matron. It opened as the Lister House Hotel in the 1930s, at roughly the same time that the Temperance Hotel, by then run by Reginald Pratt, closed its doors. Mrs Pratt ran a shop here into the 1950s; the building is now called Wellington House, possibly after the Duke of Wellington, who revolutionised the brewing industry with his Beer House Act of 1830.

Hitchin, Bridge Street.

Bridge Street

A Great Northern Railway flat wagon pauses outside the former Marshall & Pierson maltings; the maltings of the Lucas Brewery can be seen in the distance, just past the bridge. On the left is the garage of Slater Batty; this was replaced by a new garage built by R. E. Sanders in 1914, which today is the Bridge Street Bistro.

Former Royal Oak
After closure as the Royal Oak pub,
No. 27 Bridge Street was Walker's cycle
shop. Before the renumbering of the
buildings in Bridge Street, it had been
No. 14. Mr Walker, who lived in Pirton
Road, is seen standing outside the shop
in the earlier view. By the 1970s, the
building was the home of Codicote Press

Bridge Street Looking West

In the years after the Second World War, Furr's sweet shop (at No. 31) and Furr's fish shop (at No. 11) faced each other across Bridge Street. In 2014, No. 31 is now Little Roots children's hairdressers. No. 29, formerly No. 16, was the Whitehope restaurant, run by Misses White and Hope. The building lost its upper floor in the extensive renovations carried out here and at the former Royal Oak in the 1960s; the timber frame of its eastern gable is visible inside from ground to apex.

The Plough, Bridge Street

The earlier view shows the Lucas brewery's closest tied house, just across the street from the brewery complex. The building that it was replaced by closed as a pub in 1966 and is still occupied today by Bowens solicitors.

Brewery House, Sun Street

The brewery at the south end of Sun Street was established by the Draper family, who put it up alongside other buildings in 1734 as surety for a loan from William Lucas. Repayment difficulties led to the acquisition of the brewery by the Lucas family, who replaced the old properties facing Sun Street with this large house in 1780. After the closure of the brewery in 1923, the house became Philpotts furniture store until 2012. Mevan Ocakbasi & Bar opened here in 2014.

Sun Street, Middle

The jettied gable of No. 18 Sun Street contrasts with the eighteenth- and nineteenth-century frontages further up the street. The earlier view shows the gents outfitters shop of Ebenezer Allsop at No. 19; after some intervening years as a music and then antiques shop, the building became Kang's Barber Shop and has been Ali Barbers since March 2013.

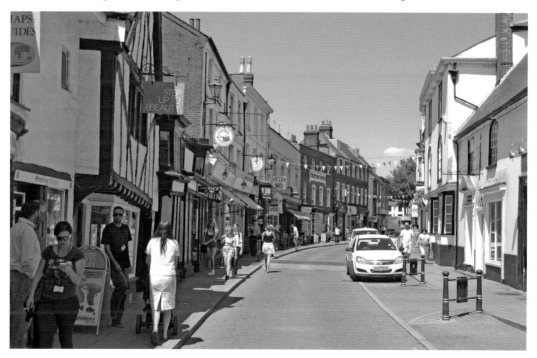

Sun Street, Looking Towards Market Place

The earlier view shows the Shell sign of Morgans Garage; as well as holding the Singer dealership, the garage charged accumulators with battery acid for radios in the days before universal mains electricity. The garage stretched all the way through to Bucklersbury, where it remains as Del Basso Bros. Today, the Sun Street frontage is a Zizzi Italian restaurant.

A Third Angel

The house at No. 5 Sun Street fronted the eighteenth-century brewery of John Crabb, later Marshall & Pierson. After the failure of Marshall & Pierson in 1841, the house was Hitchin Conservative Club for more than a century before being acquired for conversion into a J. D. Wetherspoon pub. Early in 2014, it was announced that the venture would be taking the name of the Angel Vaults. The earlier photograph, at the time of the Coronation celebrations of 1911, shows the original Angel Inn on the left, which once hosted King Henry VIII and was latterly called the Angel Vaults before demolition in 1956. A replacement pub – the Angel's Reply – was opened by brewer McMullen in 1965 along Bedford Road, which is now known as Angels, leaving the Sun Hotel to enjoy the unusual distinction of having two rivals with the same name on either of its sides within sixty years.

Jeeves, Market Place

In Hitchin, the Jeeves family was mainly associated with building and brick-making, based on their yard in Queen Street, but in the late nineteenth century they ran a draper's shop at No. 19 Market Place. For many years in the twentieth century, the premises was Curry's cycle and then a domestic appliance shop.

Market Place From Church Tower

Just over a century of change is evident in these two views. Aside from the Churchgate development of the early 1970s, many other buildings have been altered at the rear and the old vicarage (foreground) has received shopfronts.

Hospital Demonstration, 1911

Just over a fortnight after the lavish pageant to celebrate the Coronation of King George V, the town was to see another procession, this time for a hospital demonstration. With the union flags and bunting put away, the Associated Society of Locomotive Engineers and Firemen (ASLEF) float makes its way across the Market Place on 8 July 1911.

539. The Market Square, Hitchin.

Market Place, South West Corner
While all of the buildings from the Rose & Crown to the start of Sun Street were replaced in the twentieth century, those opposite, in this view, have changed only in detail.

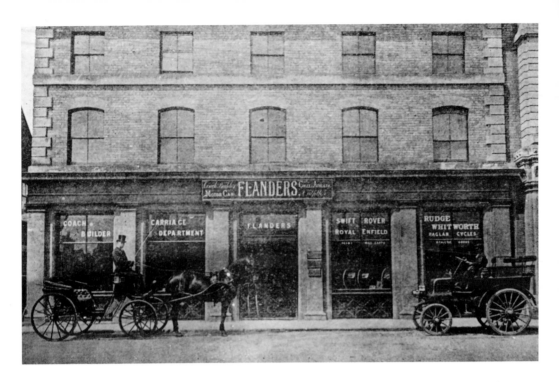

Flanders

No. 30 Market Place, built by the iron founder Thomas Perkins, occupies the site of the old Red Lion Inn. By the start of the twentieth century, the premises were run by George Flanders, who had a foot in both the horse-drawn and motor ages, specialising in carriages, bicycles and cars.

THE MARKET, HITCHIN.

Market Place, North-West Corner

The general market was held on Tuesdays in the Market Place until the start of the Second World War when the construction of a large emergency water tank to the right of the photograph prompted its 'temporary' removal to St Mary's Square.

No. 1 Market Place

The earlier view shows the attractive Queen Anne style timber-framed building at the corner of the High Street and Market Place. Lamb's drapery business had become John Jackson's draper's shop by the early twentieth century. In 1921, the building and part of the first house on the east side of the High Street were replaced by a branch of Midland Bank.

Post Office, Market Place

Prior to 1904, Hitchin's main post office was at No. 2 Market Place, since which date it has been in Brand Street, Hermitage Road, Market Place again (at No. 32 when it shared Lavell's premises) and is currently at Brookers, Bucklersbury. No. 2 was Briggs shoe shop for much of the twentieth century.

Former Red Cow
Once a Marshall & Pierson house, the Red Cow passed through the hands of Pryors of Baldock, Phillips of Royston and J. W. Green of Luton. Closing as a pub under the Whitbread/Flowers aegis in 1967, it was then part of that company's Thresher off-licence chain before being sold in the 1980s. The building dates from the second half of the seventeenth century; 1676 is cut into one of the risers of its staircase.

Former Artichoke

At one time the Artichoke pub, the earlier view shows the building during its time as Martha Flint's millinery shop. She was assisted by Ebenezer Allsop who would later be at No. 19 Sun Street (*see page 15*).

Old Houses, Church Gates
The building nearest the camera was the shop of Henry Moulden, photographer and teacher of music. He was also the organist at St Mary's church. Now part of Halseys shop, the building is open from the ground to the roof, having lost its upper floor.

St. Mary's Church, Hitchin.   Moulden, Photo, Hitchin

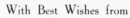

St Mary's Churchyard

Two views with the tower of St Mary's church obscured. The first view was taken during the restoration of the tower in 1906/07; since then, the lime tree has flourished.

Bucklersbury, Looking North

In the earlier view, Mr Lewin's premises at No. 28 had yet to be incorporated into the Red Hart next door. The Lewin family had many connections with Bucklersbury during the nineteenth and early twentieth centuries, including running the Red Lion. The landlord of the Red Hart in the 1930s and 1940s, 'Tony' Bongers, made his own hamburgers, which were very popular with American troops in the latter years of the Second World War.

Bucklersbury, Hitchin   27688

Bucklersbury, Looking South
The view from outside the Red Hart. The rear of Morgans Garage (*see page 16*), today Del Basso Bros, can be seen as a British Railways van negotiates its way past a Flowers dray delivering to the Kings Arms.

Tilehouse Street

A view that has changed little over the years. The former Woodman pub at the corner of Bucklersbury has had its studwork plastered over and some 'retro' street lighting has been installed, but otherwise this prospect remains remarkably unaltered.

Coopers Arms

Today's Coopers Arms is of two phases and was formerly two separate buildings, long since joined together by the addition of the section with the gabled dormer window. The gable nearest the camera is a conventional North Herts timber-framed construction, and a glance at the ceiling in the bar and gents toilet shows that it contains a dragon beam resulting from its originally being jettied on two sides. In 1911, a blacksmith, James Day, lived in the yard through the gateway.

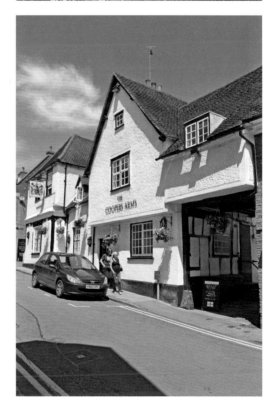

Coopers Arms Looking East

The western half of the pub is believed to originally have been the Tylers' guildhall. Of stone construction, it dates from the fifteenth century and has the remains of three three-light mullioned windows, with cinquefoil stonework picked out in black paint in the contemporary view. Three equivalent windows, almost complete, survive in the rear wall.

High Street, Hitchin.

H. G. Moulden, Photo, Hitchin.

High Street From South End

As well as being a newsagent, bookseller and printer, Montague Wakenell, whose premises are seen here at No. 3 High Street, published many postcards of Hitchin, some of which appear in these pages. This view, however, was the work of Henry Moulden, who after moving from by the Church Gates (*see page 28*) operated from the building directly opposite with the bay window.

HITCHIN, HIGH STREET.

Barclays Bank

The Italianate building of Barclays Bank at No. 5 High Street has its origins in Piersons bank of 1840. Piersons failed at the same time as the Marshall & Pierson brewery in 1841 and the bank was taken over by Sharples, Exton & Lucas, who extended the building over the site of No. 6 High Street (*far right*). From 1855, the bank was known as Sharples, Tuke, Lucas & Lucas and four years later a marriage alliance led to a change to Sharples, Tuke, Lucas & Seebohm. A further marriage connected the enterprise to the Barclay family of Lombard Street, London.

High Street, Middle

The upper view shows the High Street shortly before Perks & Llewellyn (*far left*) closed. On the right-hand side of the street, the Black Horse is still open, but has become a Flowers pub following the takeover of Fordham's brewery of Ashwell by J. W. Green of Luton in 1952.

Woolworths Under Construction

Just thirty years after much of the Cock Hotel was demolished to allow the building of a Woolworths store, the opportunity was taken to build a larger store where Perks & Llewellyn had stood. The steel frame of the new building was being assembled in November 1964.

Black Horse

Newly elected Conservative MP Nigel Fisher is being carried along the High Street past the Black Horse in 1951. Mr Fisher was conveyed in this way from the Town Hall in Brand Street to the Conservative Club in Sun Street. Sharpe's newsagents had been the White Horse, a Healey of Harpenden pub, in the nineteenth century, before passing to Youngs of Hertford and then Pryor Reid of Hatfield.

High Street, North End

John Cannon's fruitery is prominent in the earlier view; Mr Cannon ran the Chalkdell Nursery in Union Road (now Oughtonhead Way) where Westbury Close, Friday Furlong and Lower Innings are today. His son, Frank, played football for Queens Park Rangers and West Ham and was killed in action near Ypres in 1916.

Moss's Corner

Half a century after it sold its business to International Stores, the architectural legacy of the firm of W. B. Moss remains considerable. Their first substantial building, No. 13 High Street, was built in 1868 and just over thirty years later they replaced the former Trooper pub with the building now containing the Vodafone shop. With its early use of girders to produce large spans, and decorative yellow-glazed tiles and Art Nouveau mosaic panels depicting tea plants, the building still leads this location to be known as Moss's Corner.

Bancroft Livestock Market

The Tuesday livestock market was held in Bancroft until 1904, when it moved to Paynes Park. The tall house at the corner of Portmill Lane was Ansells and later Gunner's butchers. Today it is Marks & Spencer. Next door, the White Lion pub can be seen in the earlier view.

BANCROFT AND HIGH STREET, HITCHIN   H 7662

Bancroft, Looking Towards High Street

A No. 209 Birch Bros bus has arrived from Henlow Camp. This bus company was a major operator, running services to London via the Old London Road through Codicote. Obscured by the tree in the earlier view, the Guild House stands to the right.

3799 Bancroft, Hitchin.

Bancroft From Outside Moss's Furnishers

The loss of the range of buildings on the east side of Bancroft between Portmill Lane and Hermitage Road (seen here from outside Moss's household and furniture shop, now Superdrug) is still much regretted. In the distance, the chimney of Russell's tannery can be seen over the rooftops.

Bancroft, Showing The Croft
Another major loss to Bancroft was the demolition of The Croft in 1964. Its replacement units (today Morrisons, Costa coffee and the Garden House Hospice shop) did incorporate replicated features from the frontage of the old house.

Bancroft, Looking South From Hermitage Road
The older view shows Nicholls draper's with its then relatively new plate-glass windows inserted into the early nineteenth-century house. One of Hitchin's most prominent stores until the 1970s, today Nicholls is White Stuff, Monsoon and Prezzo.

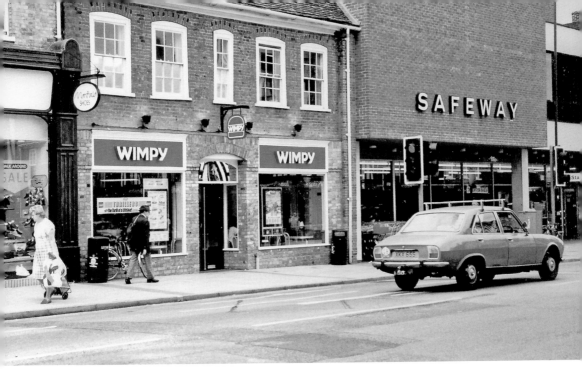

Wimpy Bar and Safeway

The mid-eighteenth-century house, which today is the location of Prezzo, was in the 1980s one of two Wimpy Bars in Hitchin (the other was on the site of the Angel Vaults in Sun Street) before becoming a Burger King outlet. The British Listed Buildings text for No. 17 Bancroft describes the premises as 'disfigured by blatant modern shop window' in a rare outburst of emotion. (*Brian Norman*)

Bancroft Showing Abbott's

The three-storey 1920s replacement for the Hermitage (*see page 50*) was for many years Abbott's furnisher's. More recently, Wallace Kings and then Clement Joscelyne were here, prior to Kenmore Interiors.

Bancroft, Looking South

With Moss's Corner looming in the distance, part of Phillips of Hitchin Antiques at the Manor House can be seen on the right. On the left-hand side of the street, the first-floor bay window of the surviving part of The Hermitage can be seen.

The Hermitage

The home of Quaker philanthropist Frederic Seebohm, The Hermitage was an eclectic mix of several buildings put together to make one of Hitchin's grandest houses. With extensive gardens stretching back to Queen Street and the point where Walsworth and Whinbush Roads begin, Seebohm was responsible for the creation of Hermitage Road, donating the ground to the town.

Bancroft, East Side

Nos 103 and 104 Bancroft were once used as a store by Phillips of Hitchin. The upper floor of No. 105 was formerly used for board meetings by William Ransom & Son.

Russells

One of the town's major employers in the twentieth century was the tannery of G. W. Russell & Son. Together with the pharmaceutical firm of Willam Ransom and the electric power station, Russell's works created an industrial area in the low-lying land between Bancroft and Whinbush Road. Russells closed down here in 1987, but the business continues to this day as Russells Fine Leathers, run from Wilby in Suffolk, but still with a presence in Hitchin; the earlier view shows the entrance from Bancroft in the 1980s before the site was redeveloped into Sainsbury's supermarket. (*Brian Norman*)

Skynner Almshouses

The Skynner Almshouses result from two bequests from the Skynner family. John Skynner bequeathed funds in 1666 to provide houses for eight married couples; thirty years later, Ralph Skynner bequeathed £800 to build and endow eight further homes, which were built in 1698. The houses were remodelled in the 1960s.

Bancroft Recreation Ground Tennis Courts

The tennis courts at Bancroft Recreation Ground have been a feature of the gardens since they were opened at the end of the 1920s. At the time of writing, a remodelling scheme is proposed to reduce the number of courts from seven to three. Other tennis courts in the town have been at the Sun Hotel and the former Hitchin Lawn Tennis Club courts at Lister Avenue; there is a single public tennis court at King George V Playing Field.

Bancroft Recreation Ground, Hitchin   27682

Bancroft Recreation Ground Entrance

The north-west corner of Bancroft Recreation Ground. The Starlings Bridge development on the site of the Hitchin Gas Co. works can be seen in the contemporary photograph.

Welcome to
Bancroft Gardens
For any enquiries phone 01462 474000

BRAND STREET, HITCHIN. H.7658

Brand Street From the High Street

Sixty years separate these two views showing the south side of Brand Street. In the 1950s, the Post Office pensions (opposite the main post office) occupied what is now Stonegate Estates, while Chesham House (now Southern Fried Chicken and Jules) was still a private house.

V. H. Garratt, Fishmonger & Poulterer, Hitchin.

Garratts

An impressive display in 1911 from the shop of V. H. Garratt. Today, the premises have been incorporated into NatWest bank.

Brand Street From Bedford Road

The view down Brand Street from the start of Bedford Road. The original town hall (now Ivory) dominates the right-hand side of the street. This was built in 1840 and was designed by architect Thomas Bellamy. Bellamy had designed the Hitchin Infirmary, which was built the previous year. This building, just yards away in Bedford Road behind the camera, has now taken the name Thomas Bellamy House.

The Town Hall, Hitchin.

Town Hall

The Old Town Hall was soon found to be too small and in 1898 plans were hatched for a new building on land donated by Alfred Ransom and Frederic Seebohm. Opened in 1901, the building was designed by Edward Mountford and T. Geoffry Lucas (of the Hitchin brewing family) in Neo-Georgian 'Wrenaissance' style. For three months in 1913, while rebuilding of Blakes Picturedrome (*see page 67*) was being undertaken, the Town Hall was used by the Blake brothers as a temporary cinema. At the time of writing, the building was being converted in a £4.39-million scheme to provide a district museum, replacing the now-closed Hitchin Museum in Paynes Park and the Letchworth Museum & Art Gallery, which was set to open in June 2015.

The Dog

Once a tied house of the Bucklersbury Brewery, The Dog, along with the H. A. Saunders (formerly Chalkleys) garage and the Methodist church, was replaced by a Sainsbury's supermarket in 1974. The building is now occupied by Argos and New Look.

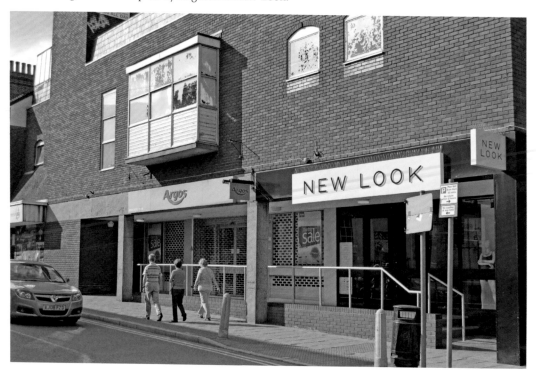

BUTT'S CLOSE, HITCHIN

Butts Close, South-West Corner

The ancient open space of Butts Close is bound on two sides by Bedford Road. Today, the concrete posts have weathered somewhat and the buildings of the northern arm of Bedford Road are largely obscured by trees.

Butts Close, Looking North

While cows no longer graze on Butts Close as in the earlier view, common grazing rights still exist. Top Field, in the distance across Fishponds Road, is the home of Hitchin Town Football Club, although in recent years plans have been put forward to build a supermarket on the site.

Fearless and Gun, Butts Close

The name of Butts Close refers to the historical use of the ground for archery practice; indeed, Henry VIII practised archery here. More modern forms of warfare were marked between the wars when a tank, *Fearless* (No. 2088), and German Howitzer gun were placed at the north-west corner of Butts Close. Sadly, unlike neighbours Baldock and Stevenage, Hitchin does not have a street fair, but fairs continue to visit Butts Close.

Burford Ray
The northern boundary of the parish of Hitchin is provided by the River Oughton, over which the Bedford Road passes at Burford Ray. Today, the bridge has been widened along with the road and the riverbank is rather more overgrown.

Royal Engineers Depot

During the First World War, a Royal Engineers signal depot camp was set up on land alongside Bedford Road. The guard house was Bearton Lodge on the corner of Bearton Road, whose gable is visible in the earlier view. Some of the land remains in military use, under the Bearton Camp name, as the base for Hitchin Sea Cadets and the Hitchin Detachment of the Bedfordshire & Hertfordshire Army Cadet Force, as well as being the Territorial Army centre. Frank Young Court, commemorating Hitchin's holder of the Victoria Cross, is also on the site of the Royal Engineers base (*inset*), from which a contemporary view of the northern gable of Bearton Lodge is just possible.

WILSHERE-DACRE SCHOOL, HITCHIN.

Wilshere Dacre School

Taking its name from William Wilshere and Lord Dacre, founders of the British Schools in Queen Street, the school in Fishponds Road opened in 1929. Originally for junior and senior pupils, today it is a junior school.

Ickleford Road

The south end of Ickleford Road has been dominated by the building that was Hitchin's first cinema for nearly a century. Established in 1911 at No. 98 Ickleford Road, Blakes Picturedrome was soon rebuilt with a very grand frontage. The opening of the lavishly appointed Hermitage Cinema in 1932 provided some stiff competition and when, in 1939, the Regal Cinema opened in Bancroft, the Picturedrome closed. Today, the site of the Picturedrome is the Royal Quarter apartment development, but an imposing frontage with three arches has been maintained. The site of the houses next door, Nos 96 and 97, is now used for access to Hitchin Police Station.

St Michaels College

Originating in France, St Michaels College, run by the Edmundian Fathers, moved to Hitchin in 1903 and completed this impressive building in 1906, seen before the addition of a new wing in 1919. The school moved to Stevenage in 1968 and has now been incorporated into the co-educational Catholic John Henry Newman School. The Hitchin building, after use as an annexe for Hitchin College of Further Education, was demolished in 1971.

Roman Catholic Church

Seen above in its original form prior to the addition of a bell tower in 1907, the Catholic church of Our Lady Immaculate and St Andrew was built in 1901 at the corner of Grove and Nightingale Roads.

Frythe Cottages, Nightingale Road

The junction between Ickleford and Nightingale Roads. Nos 1–4 Nightingale Road – Frythe Cottages – were built in the early nineteenth century and are the oldest buildings in a street that only started to be developed in earnest after the coming of the railway.

Nightingale Road, Hitchin.

Nightingale Road

With the photographer standing at the point where the River Hiz passes under Starlings Bridge, the Woolpack pub can be seen on the right with its two bay windows. Blacksmith William Berridge operated a forge at the Woolpack Yard, which remained until 1959. The site of the Woolpack is now redeveloped for housing with the building line set back somewhat.

Starlings Place and Verulam Road

The buildings that are today the Punjab Balti were in the 1950s Burdett's fur shop and Wilkinson's general stores. The Territorials Club, between Verulam and Whinbush Roads, with its drill hall to the rear, gave way to Hitchin Trades & Labour Club. Today, the site is the home of Club 85, renowned in Hitchin and beyond for its concerts by nationally known as well as local bands.

Whinbush Road

The last but one group of thatched houses near the centre of Hitchin were these cottages in Whinbush Road. Today, their site is occupied by the Elderflower Court flats. The very last thatched houses in the town, Nos 19 and 20 Florence Street, were destroyed by fire in the late twentieth century.

Walsworth Road Baptist Church
Originally a modest tin building on the site of the church hall (nearest the camera), Walsworth Road Baptist church was constructed in 1875. The church hall was built by the Queen Street firm of Jeeves in 1914.

Walsworth Road, Hitchin.

Walsworth Road, Looking North

Walsworth Road was called Station Road in the late nineteenth century. The building at the corner of Radcliffe Road, today Nisa local, was Walsworth Road sub-post office and in 1878 was referred to as 'Station Road branch office'.

The Concrete House, Walsworth Road
While Hitchin abounds with fine houses of all periods from late-medieval onwards, perhaps the most remarkable is No. 47 Walsworth Road. Built in the 1860s of concrete, it was at the time of the earlier view Tabner's Dining Rooms. By 1929, the business was listed as 'W. M. Tabner, Temperance Hotel' and was still going strong in 1937.

Walsworth Road, Looking Towards Town Centre

Today, the gated development of Rose Cottage Gardens has been built on the site of No. 89 Walsworth Road to the left of this view. The buildings opposite remain unchanged, with the business of Pepper, the monumental masons, having been here since the late nineteenth century.

On the Down Platform

The opening of the Great Northern Railway (GNR) changed Hitchin forever: the town expanded from its centre towards the railway and the railway station was rebuilt in 1910. The old postcard shows Benslow Bridge and an impressive signal gantry in the distance. In 2014, rebuilt 'West Country' class locomotive No. 34046 *Braunton* hurries past with the 'White Rose II' train for York.

THE STATION, HITCHIN.

Down Platform From Up Platform

The earlier view of the Down platform shows Hitchin Yard signal box and the GNR goods shed just beyond the end of the platform. The lofty prospect of the signal box is thought to result from the footbridge that spanned the tracks before the station subway was dug as part of the station rebuilding.

GNR Goods Warehouses
The GNR goods yard had two warehouses
to the west of the goods shed. One was
demolished in 1997, but the other remains.

Radcliffe Road
The view north from Walsworth Road. St Saviour's church was built by the Revd George Gainsford, who purchased the site and paid for its construction himself. The church was consecrated in May 1865 and is a motif of the town's railway-age expansion.

Benslow

Benslow Lane is redolent with cultural connections. It was here, at what is now Benslow Nursing Home, that the College for Women (which went on to become Cambridge University's Girton College) was founded in 1869. The Victorian house Fairfield, at Little Benslow Hills, became a world-renowned centre for musical instruction.

Chiltern Road
While the trees in the roadway of Hermitage Road (*see page 86*) are long gone, the same arrangement persists in Chiltern Road, part of the Nettledell Estate

The Avenue
The south end of The Avenue, looking north from the junction with Wymondley Road.

WINDMILL HILL, HITCHIN.

Windmill Hill
If Hermitage Road and Queen Street have changed significantly in the past century, Windmill Hill has not. The open land was given to the town by Frederic Seebohm's daughters in 1921.

Hermitage Road

With white-painted trees suggesting that the photograph dates from the days of blackout during the First World War, Hermitage Road is seen before the interwar development began. Barker's barns, which would later be at the side of the widened road, can be seen through the trees.

Hermitage Cinema

The largest and most opulent of Hitchin's cinemas, the Hermitage, opened in 1932 complete with orchestra pit, proper stage and dressing rooms for theatrical productions. The Hitchin Thespians performed here many times, staging *Showboat* in 1939 with a cast of nearly 100. Closure came in 1963, the year after the new main post office building, with a sorting office behind, was opened next door.

Hollow Lane and Windmill Hill

As part of the changes to the area that accompanied the creation of St Mary's Square and the clearing away of many densely packed dwellings around Queen Street, Hollow Lane was remodelled, and St Andrews Street lost its separate identity. A new road, Mount Garrison, was made, and retaining walls of black iron slag were erected along the roadside. These steps were installed in 1931.

View From Windmill Hill

The earlier view shows the telephone exchange dating from 1955 alongside Hollow Lane before its major expansion in 1973. The 1960s flats of Woodcote House are also yet to be built.

Portmill Lane

No longer a through road into Bancroft today, the Portmill Lane of the 1950s is seen in the earlier view. The two houses on the right were the offices of Hawkins & Co., solicitors. It was here that the young Reginald Hine spent countless afternoons perusing old documents as he researched his groundbreaking books on Hitchin history. As Hawkins Russell Jones, the firm was able to boast that it was the second oldest legal practice in the country, having been founded by John Skynner in 1591. Hawkins Russell Jones was created by a merger in 1987; in 2009 this firm merged with Foreman Laws of Welwyn Garden City to create HRJ Foreman Laws, which vacated the Portmill Lane building but still has a presence in Hitchin at No. 25 Bancroft.

The River Hiz

As part of the St Mary's Square scheme, the River Hiz was straightened out as it passed St Mary's church. The earlier view shows Moss's warehouse in Portmill Lane and, with the large windows of the Hermitage Halls on the north side of Hermitage Road visible, must date from before the construction of the Hermitage Cinema, which began in 1931.

THE BIGGIN, HITCHIN.

The Biggin Courtyard
The south-west corner of the Biggin courtyard. The building was originally a Gilbertine priory dating from 1361 but was extensively rebuilt in the seventeenth century, when it became a complex of almshouses.

Inside the Biggin

The Biggin has been managed by Messrs John Shilcock for the trustees since 1840. Today, its residents are public sector employees such as teachers and health workers, rather than elderly poor women as before. Robbie Yon occupies a part of the complex where the unnamed lady in the earlier photograph lived around 1903.

Biggin Garret

At least two postcards were produced of the attics of the Biggin at the start of the twentieth century. These views are taken inside the attic of the eastern range of the building just over 110 years apart. An extensive collection of graffiti, dating back to the nineteenth century and including many Hitchin 'names', as well as Antipodean soldiers during the First World War, testifies to many people's interest in this fascinating building.

Queen Street

Today's Queen Street retains only its more respectable buildings after the clearances of ninety years ago. While these timber-framed premises just in front of today's bus stop L were quite charming, there were the seventeen closely-packed houses of Chapmans Yard through the gateway, stretching all the way down to the River Hiz, with hardly any sanitary provision.

View From Cemetery Gates

Hitchin Cemetery was opened in 1857 on the high ground off St John's Road overlooking the town from the south-east. The building of Nursery Hill and tree growth prevents the original view from being replicated exactly, but the roofs of the British Schools buildings in Queen Street are readily identifiable in both photographs.